An Amaltas in Mumbai

Suparna Gupta

BookLeaf
Publishing

India | USA | UK

Presentation by *BookLeaf Publishing*

Web: www.bookleafpub.com

E-mail: info@bookleafpub.com

ISBN: 9789360948887

First edition 2024

For Ma

Staying Home

I suggest you don't set a plate for me
at your dinner table of eight and please
don't wait for me at a theatre or gallery
because I am staying at home waiting for
sadness
to hit me in a way that is recognisable as pain or
anguish
I have been reading about loss and how it is
sheer agony
eager for some clarity about how it should feel
I googled sorrow late last night and found
synonyms like misery and despair
both of which I believe I could bear
perhaps even prefer to this woozy woolly weight
that has settled heavily keeping me still and safe
from bumping into spiky-edged pain which
might draw blood
and drip onto the carpet below
while I stay home and wait for sorrow

An Amaltas in Mumbai

an Amaltas tree grows
sweetly in the shadow
of the grand city museum
where ancient sculptures and antiquities reside
the museum guide talks with great pride
about a brand new exhibit
he tells story after story
about military might and glory,
and legendary strength and beauty
while in the garden the Amaltas blooms
because it is her duty
to flower yellow and bright
for those who need wisdom and light
on a particularly dark and moonless night

Florida State Driving License

I will confess
I have often stopped to wonder
about the non-value
of some things you left to me
like your non-need for holidays
that made me a non-traveler,
a non-tourist a non-trekker
non-lover of pristine beaches
and green rolling hills
non-seeker of sky-diving thrills
a naysayer spirit grown and watered
in a childhood too small and sheltered
were you never preparing us
for bigger things at all
then weeks after you are gone
I find your Florida State driving license
with a photo of your dazzling smile
tinged with a hint of non-belonging
non-revealing of daily aches or longing
for a different life
a quieter softer one perhaps
as non-mother or non-wife

we celebrated your license
with vanilla milkshakes
you drove three miles light years from home

to give us a treat but your non-enjoyment
of the drink sweet and wonderfully cold
told us this was a non-celebration
of a non-life of a person on-hold
no matter how bold or non-lost you seemed
uprooted and placed in somebody else's dream
no doubt it took guts for you to decide
to give up your license to drive
on roads that lead to a sparkling new life
yet you returned to India in too short a time
to a non-starter plan a bit past your prime
to claim you were deeply satisfied
with a quick taxi ride to Strand Bookstore
or Colaba silver market next door
did it take courage to stay a non-believer
of the idea that life always has to be more
to choose the role of a non-adventurer
who came back to a home you adore

In Your Hands

they say if you look deep into your hands
you will see your ancestors
and the curves of head and heart
hold a gold mine of secrets
whispered into palms over generations
broken and unbroken lines
are age-old bonds and ties
the mystic cross on both our palms
are signs that time after time
life after life we are connected
through bodies minds or bloodlines
as fathers and sons sisters and brothers
in a myriad other ways
we find our way to each other
to give the love left over to give
to live the life left over to live together

Messaged

it is almost the end
things that must be said have been said
heart and time slow down
I ask for a message and on cue
my phone beeps
I can't let go of your hand or you
for too many reasons
with one hand I riffle through my purse
two more beeps from the universe
otp otp otp
messages admonish impatiently
I reply five two three three
and glance at your flattening ecg
my mind now full of trivialities
Amazon deliveries the week's groceries
bank transfers and month-end salaries
a dull to-do list cold and mundane in this
moment
yet somehow kind in its horrible sense of
normalcy

Oven Demo

the salesman arrived for his home visit and
demo
his boss had recently issued another memo
saying homemakers were goddesses who
shouldn't have to wait
to put the finest food on family plates
the demo began smoothy and he was pointing to
the grill
when he observed the oven-owner had gone very
still
start again she barked with a scowl and a frown
an oven shouldn't be as difficult as this sounds
he explained again and did yet another encore
after which he repeated himself a few times
more
she asked if engineers at Siemens had gone mad
this is more complicated than any appliance I've
had
ours is the Mercedes of ovens he replied
the best chefs choose it he beamed with pride
more furious she spouted words that made no
sense
how ovens by Siemens were designed to rob
self-confidence
that she had led an organisation over two
decades

won many awards and several accolades
only after her mother's recent passing had she
set a new goal
to take on and master a new home-maker role
as a feminist and a leader she refused to break
or be beaten by a cake that just wouldn't bake
his smile was kind as he heard her critique
I'm so sorry for your loss he said and before she
could speak
left her home promising to reschedule for next
week
at the sales team meet he talked about why he
had run
as an oven expert you must know when things
are raw or done
his boss previously peeved he hadn't completed
that demo
was so impressed with this thought he wrote it
up as a new memo

Pencil It In

may we pencil in a minute to just fall apart
to wail and scream at jagged cuts to the heart
could we smash a vase of flowers straight to the
ground
fling dinner plates at walls and scatter shards
around
should we declare aloud we're at the edge on the
brink
end polite silences to say what we actually think
should we break positivity rules, crack and fall
unload kilos of negative baggage to just express
it all
this month on our calendars can we mark a
cracked heart
dedicate time to rage and slash some elegant art
rip out pages of exquisite novels with bare hands
throw away good taste and see where we land
should we delay wholesome hikes and
himalayan holidays
dive deep inward to drown in a murky pain-haze
if calendars are full till the second thursday in
may
could we pencil in a quick minute now simply to
say
we are broken we are lost things are far from
okay.

Afterwards

how a mighty storm leaves
the world lying on its side
like an injured animal that heaves
in pain through the night
hours later grit-filled eyes open
to rain-washed sights
and a terribly ordinary
watery morning light

Insomnia

what wakes you up in the dark
why does sleep feel frail
is it starlight from a future dream
too brilliant to be real
or vague unease from a sickle moon
ghostly and too pale
Is it streaks of inspiration like a comet's
brilliant burning trail
or does doubt sneak in soon after midnight
asking if you did perfectly right by those
who lived for you or did you perhaps fail

Flotsam

Like a drawer full of important things
overflowing
a blur of people, eyes soft and knowing
barely registered faces, but arms full of care
we spot signs of comfort everywhere
in peeled orange segments, a healing prayer
an overnight case of someone
who rushed in from a faraway place
in midnight words and fragrant flowers
in home-made meals and tupperware jars
but the water level is rising so it's time to admit
defeat
the tide is not turning and the water will not
retreat
when the giant wave crashes in anchoring no
longer matters
swept away beside the hospital bed
we are slammed down and battered
hopes tattered hearts spattered when our eyes
open at dawn everyone is long gone
our heads still under water we're more alone
than we can bear
till we spot wispy signs of comfort
still floating there in the air
peeled orange segments a healing prayer
an overnight case of someone

who rushed in from a faraway place
midnight words and fragrant flowers
home-made meals in tupperware jars
things we lost and found again
now tangled and knotted into our pain
we emerge unsteady on shaky ground
odds and ends to do with love
like flotsam floating all around

The Bear from Guatemala

you might think a mother's last words
would be profound and wise
but she spoke to both daughters about a bear
from Guatemala much to their surprise
she also left some cryptic clues
though they couldn't quite tell what for
both sisters followed her hints obediently
to reach their mother's front door
then down a narrow passage
they took a left into her room until
they got to a drawer of old papers
searched among files and bills
found a box hand-painted in blue
went right past her final will
to retrieve a key hoping to see
the striped toy where it always used to be

at last their mother's cupboard door opened
they felt her presence everywhere
among clothes and jewelry
her fragrance hung densely in the air
her playful smiling voice was clear
as if she was still standing there
through a handwritten note she had kept
in the striped pocket of the bear
I just wanted the three of us to enjoy

one final wild goose chase today
so when both of you are together
you never forget how to play
you might think a mother's final advice would
be serious
she should have weighty words to share
but this child's sweet lesson
kissed them lightly and floated up into the air

Jokes

I wish we had a song we had named our own
so that every time the tune plays
my memories could dance along
what if we had decided on a secret code or
phrase
a spell to transport me to a childhood place
ever nurturing ever safe
we should have chosen a secret recipe
which tastes of comfort smells of spice and
family
instead we chose to have silly inside jokes that
provoke
unreasonably loud laughter that make me choke,
catch my throat
and make my eyes burn

I Miss Nothing

there is nothing to miss this morning
some-time between nine thirty and ten
our daily three-person call
was hardly time well-spent, even then
headlines usually glossed over
little international or local news
literary sparkle barely fussed over
the rare debate on world issues

there is nothing to miss this morning
conversations always too light
few rules about family duty
or discussion about wrong and right
hardly much instruction
teaching typically cast aside
small things of no consequence
few efforts to mentor or guide

what is worth talking about this morning
important things are over and done
who cares about things like a nip in the air
hair-setting gel for grey flyaway hair
food parcels to be refrigerated at once
plans to invite old school-mates for lunch
children's homework left incomplete
or construction noise taking over the street

so there is nothing to miss this morning
the window of insignificant chatter
too easily replaced by people and plans
or grander things that greatly matter
until a tiny trivial thought emerges
too small and unimportant to say
swallowed silently, it waits painfully unspoken
for those most- ordinary minutes of the day

Hawaiian Night

I too imagined myself married by the age of
twenty or thirty
from my wise eight-year-old view that's what
old people do
have a child maybe two and by that time I
assumed
I would become exactly like you

I too would think of myself with hair twisted
into a low-braided bun
dressed in silk sarees of peacock greens and
blues
and wrapped in six yards of elegance I knew
I could greatly resemble you

I too would be gracious and perfect
in my ten-year-old mind, grace was loosely
defined
as just being fine with all kinds of things and
people
who would say about me ah the apple didn't fall
far from the tree

but I didn't get your open smile, nor your
elegant sharp nose

I didn't grow into you at least not in any way
that shows
but wearing your wine-red lipstick sometimes
got me somewhat close
So I would wear Hawaiian Night Shade 302 and
try to become a bit more like you

Listen to Grass

a stone pierced the sole of my foot
it was tiny but found the centre
the most tender part
I looked down to see
newly mowed-ground
bare of the baby-soft grass
that once grew silently

Were You Kind

where was your kindness when
she needed the spotlight
to shine just for one night
were you kind
when she gained weight or lost sheen
sat alone at home became a has-been
rarely needed barely seen
when she had nothing to give and no money to
spend
did you soothe her when she failed yet again
did you look in the mirror and speak kindly to
her
in the same gentle voice you use for a friend

Little Life

group photographs of shiny people
dancing at your wedding
a radiant glow and baby bumps that grow
into smart adults
comet careers launched
from a home decorated in earth tones
often filled with food and new friends
who might mispronounce your name
or old ones who don't find you amidst the throng
till their elbows knock askew a painting
that doesn't quite belong on the main wall
in the large home of your little life.

Cells

they say I am progressing well
through the seven stages of grief
they say it is the natural trajectory
of people recently bereaved
though I find it hard to believe
there will be any kind of reprieve
people with psychology degrees
say we could live relatively pain-free
but most men who wrote the theory
didn't really know me, nor my people
they never met a man in a village of Gaya
so thirsty he went crazy in the heat
when temperatures touched fifty
but Jung understood
how that man lives in my cell memory
and how my grief will simply seep
into blood bones and cells
and while I am asleep I will keep
and deepen love's precious scars
they will cover my body with signs
that our cells keep us forever intertwined

Mehrangarh

of course I thought about you as I walked up to
the fort to the music festival in february
it was exactly the kind of night you would have
discussed with great delight
decades after it happened
the electric energy of Bhimsen Joshi years ago
when he sang till dawn
to end with Bhairav sweet and sublime as the
sun climbed high
into a warm sky
of course I imagined sitting next to both of you
at winter concerts
but the seat was never really mine to reserve nor
my traditon to preserve
although I was always welcome to join
because the melodies I heard
with my ears
both of you absorbed through every pore
minds open hearts full souls stirred
and perhaps for that reason I instinctively knew
the music season belonged
just to the two of you
of course I heard the husk in the singer's
slightly-hoarse voice
but I ignored it when I recognized her choice of
a spring raag you loved

and though it was not her finest night on stage
this time her sound went deep inside past the
tightness in my throat
far back in time then glided across lightly chilled
air
to settle on the empty chair in front of me so you
were right there making sure I could share
the end of the music season with you

Postcard from Mehrangarh

she sang for a dearest one with a weird gut-wail
that made me cringe and want to turn away
from Radha's raw devotion and pain
a deep midnight love awake in the dark
much too big to be contained
her music reminded me of a baul dance
you taught two children of five and seven
who didn't know much about the divine or
heaven
except a song about Vrindavan they were to
perform
at a pujo celebration
on imaginary ektara strings they strummed along
wandering barefoot through the room's forests
and towns
dancing around you they circled their world
singing about a divine love too great
and too unconditional to reciprocate

Women I Know

I met a woman who never asked or knew
where her husband went for official tours
one whose parents asked her to leave home
and ignored her worst childhood fears
one who rarely touched the man she adored
and one who secretly loved the girl next door
another one who never cried
after her nine-month-old stillborn baby arrived
I met a woman who laughed too hard
and one who smiled too often and too wide
lately when I have been seeing them around
without a single word or sound I've found
they speak to me I know them all well I know
the kind of stories they will tell
grandmothers aunts cousins and sisters they are
strangers
so familiar I know with certainty they are family
with an uncanny unmistakable likeness to me